APPOINTED TIMES

APPOINTED TIMES

RICHARD PRAYSON

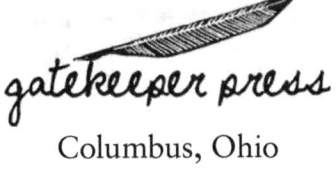
Columbus, Ohio

This book is a work of fiction. The names, characters and events in this book are the products of the author's imagination or are used fictitiously. Any similarity to real persons living or dead is coincidental and not intended by the author.

Appointed Times

Published by Gatekeeper Press
2167 Stringtown Rd, Suite 109
Columbus, OH 43123-2989
www.GatekeeperPress.com

Copyright © 2020 by Richard Prayson
All rights reserved. Neither this book, nor any parts within it may be sold or reproduced in any form or by any electronic or mechanical means, including information storage and retrieval systems without permission in writing from the author. The only exception is by a reviewer, who may quote short excerpts in a review.

The editorial work for this book is entirely the product of the author. Gatekeeper Press did not participate in and is not responsible for any aspect of that element.

ISBN (paperback): 9781642375749

To my wife Beth and my children Brigid, Nick and Diana
and to my parents Karen and Richard

"There is an appointed time for everything,
    and a time for every affair under the heaven.
A time to be born, and a time to die;
    a time to plant, and a time to uproot the plant.
A time to kill, and a time to heal;
    a time to tear down, and a time to build.
A time to weep, and a time to laugh;
    a time to mourn, and a time to dance.
A time to scatter stones, and a time to gather them;
    a time to embrace, and a time to be far from embraces.
A time to seek, and a time to lose;
    a time to keep, and a time to cast away.
A time to rend, and a time to sew;
    a time to be silent, and a time to speak.
A time to love, and a time to hate;
    a time of war, and a time of peace."

Ecclesiastes 3: 1-8

Appointed Times

O'er measured and marked sundry ways,
    by seasons, moments and by days.
        Each appointed is in its proper place,
            whether familiar or unbeknownst to grace.
Each day's light is marked by dawn,
    and which later melts with light withdrawn.
Each daylight heralds possibilities to be,
    and each night the dreams of what we can not see.
A while passes to labor and toil away,
    and then to squander free the cares of that day.
Interludes extraordinaire, momentous and so great,
    and juxtaposed with what rings ordinary and sedate.
Of memories past forlorn and blithe,
    and to move that which has yet to come with lithe.
Aspirations, expectant, wished and hoped,
    and moments with prayers heard eloped.
Out upon the snowed slopes to journey and seek,
    and when upon the distant sight arises the peak.
To entreat and inquire as we trek upon our road,
    and then to realize what was hidden as we strode.
Lives roamed and wandered faraway and near,
    and then to happenstance at once upon a place so clear.
The want to sometimes share the burdens and the yokes borne,
    and then at remaining times to want to struggle forlorn.

To spare and save what meagre amount in hand,
    and then to spend and squander riches quite unplanned.
With grievous tears that cascade from worry and from pain,
    and whilst they cry to hold and console the wounded soul's strain.
To fall and ail, transgress and err,
    and then to rise above and triumph there.
O'er marked and measured sundry ways,
    by times, occasions and by days.
        Each appointed is in its proper place,
            whether familiar or unbeknownst to grace.

Time to be Born

The night was dark,
    darker than usual it seemed,
    as he peered up toward the heavens.
He felt quite alone that night,
    all alone, as the winds blew around and through him,
    reminding him of his loves lost,
    and the pain of holding her gentle hand as she let go,
    as she breathed her last,
    also releasing hold on their son,
    who had been just born but never cried.
The sky was ceilinged by clouds,
    which seemed to race with reason toward the west,
    and he felt, as he stood,
    that he too was moving with them.
In between the shifting shape of the clouds,
    he noticed a light,
    one which seemed curiously bright,
    but blurred though his eyes' water.
He was not so sure what to make of the star,
    but it caught him,
    and held him.
And as the clouds continued to move,
    they seemed to skirt it,
    almost in deference to its luminescence.

Was it new?
He had not seen such a light that bright,
    poised in the eastern sky before.
He wiped the water with his tunic,
    to see things more clearly.
Or, was it just brighter,
    given the darkness of that night?
The glowing seemed to beckon,
    to hold his attention,
    and for the moment,
    he set aside the anguish.
Why did he notice it?
Was it real?
The spirits of the night sometimes play tricks.
Under the cloak of the night,
    they move and shift with the winds,
    and only the stars overhead,
    protected one from losing the way.
They were the truth,
    ever there,
    immutable,
    ever faithful,
    despite feeble attempts of the conspiring clouds and winds to hide them.
As he walked back to his abode,
    he kept glancing back at the light,
    checking to see if it still shone,
    in its same space,
    with its same brilliance,
    as it had.
And each time he looked,
    steady it shone.

In his slumbers,
    he restless lay,
    and dreamt of his loves lost,
    alive,
    and running somewhere, in the dark.
And after them, he chased,
    pleading,
    and begging,
    to wait for him to come.
And in the dark, up and ahead,
    he saw the light,
Clearly burning in the night overhead,
    and toward it they ran.
With the sun's rising,
    came the day,
    during which time he waited,
    for the sun's setting and the night,
    to see if it were true,
    and not a dream.
The sky on that night was clear,
    and all the stars were lit,
    set in the firmament as they were.
Toward the east, he cast his gaze,
    and there, the light was,
    as bright and as clear as the night before.
With nothing further keeping him
    where he was at the moment,
    he decided to set out toward the star,
    to perhaps find what he had lost,
    or perhaps something new.
How far the star would take him,
    he did not know.

Where it would lead him,
    he was not certain.
What he would find below where it shone,
    he had no knowledge.
He packed all his belongings,
    that which he could carry,
    and with him, also, a small vial of sweet myrrh,
    he had remaining,
    to remind him of his loves.
They would be with him,
    come with him.
And toward the star in the east he rode,
    for many a day,
    through the winds and the heat,
    and dangers unknown.
He met others along the way,
    whom the star's light had also found,
    and by its light,
    they were guided,
    toward its truth.
For with them was the faith,
    to believe in what they did not know,
    and the courage to make the journey.

A Piece of Wood

The day was like any other day,
    he thought,
    as he walked his way back,
    toward his labor.
The sun beat down as it usually wont.
The air dry as was the usual.
The street bustled with people,
    more than the usual.
He covered his face with a veil.
His skin was dark,
    and he desperately wanted to hide,
    to not be noticed as he went,
    to not see the stares,
    to not see people veer slightly to avoid him,
    to not hear the disparaging murmurs.
As he turned a corner that ordinary day,
    hiding as he walked,
    he became aware that his way was blocked.
People were lined across his way,
    some murmuring,
    some shouting,
    some watching,
    something,
    someone.
He tried to make his way around the crowds,
    but every way was impeded.

He would be late, he worried.
He must find a way to cross.
He approached and tried to make a way through,
    and was pushed, and cussed and scowled at.
The noise grew louder.
Whatever was happening was approaching.
The commotion swelled,
    as the spectacle came closer.
By some fortune, he was pushed to the front.
He wanted to continue through to the opposite side,
    toward where he was headed,
    toward where he was supposed to go,
    but realized he would have to wait
    until the procession passed.
He then noticed the man.
The man walked so slowly.
He was in a hurry.
The man fell.
There was screaming, shouting.
This would take some time,
    more time than he had.
He would be chastised for being late.
The man was not rising very quickly.
He glanced across the road to gauge the distance.
He could make it across.
He moved,
    as the man,
    ever so slowly,
    tried to stand,
    awkwardly,
    trying to balance the beam upon his shoulders.
He ran across.

He reached the opposite side and was repelled by the crowd,
	back toward the road.
Some people shouted at him,
	anger redirected toward him with features foreign.
He tried again,
	and was pushed back.
He fell in the road, as the man finally stood up.
He got up to try again,
	and as he moved, someone reached out and grabbed him.
"Have this one carry it. The man will never make it there."
"It will take too long at this rate if he keeps falling."
"Let the slave carry it."
"Yes, he is made to carry things."
He stood frozen,
	now pulled toward the center of the drama.
He would be late for certain,
	and would lose his work.
Confused, he stood,
	as the beam was lifted from the back of the man,
	and tied to his back,
	and he was told to walk.
He felt the heat of the sun and of the crowd beat on him,
	as he moved slowly along the way,
	for he had to go slowly,
	ever so slowly,
	since the man could not keep up,
	the man whose clothes were torn and bloodied,
	whose head was rimmed in blood and sweat.
He did not know the man,
	nor did he have the time to carry the beam.
The man must be a criminal,
	must have done something very wrong,

something bad,
    to be so tortured and humiliated.
The people lining the way seemed to know the man.
The man must have done something despicable,
    to be so known.
The beam's weight grew heavy,
    as he approached the hill,
    and as the crowds remained assembled at the base,
    he was forced to carry the beam up the incline,
    to where the main beam stood,
    reaching toward the sky.
Clouds move in to cover the sun,
    and a slight breeze could be felt on the rise.
At the top,
    the beam was lifted from his back,
    and hoisted with the man attached toward the heavens.
He looked up at the man,
    whose face was now visible above him.
For a brief moment,
    it appeared to him that the man looked down at him,
    and said something,
    the words of which he could not hear,
    but its meaning seemed ever so clear.
And as the sky darkened,
    there, he stood,
    with only a few others who were allowed to stand near,
    until the man shouted something,
    and then, gave up his spirit.
At that moment,
    it seemed as if the earth beneath him shook,
    and for some indescribable reason,
    he felt he could not move,

until after they pierced the dead man's side with a spear,
and pulled him down from the height.
A few men wrapped the body,
    and carried it down from the hill,
    leaving behind him
    and the beam on the ground.
As the night descended,
    he approached the beam,
    and with his hands,
    splintered off a piece of wood from the timber,
    which he and the man had carried that day,
    the day that was like no other day.

To Plant

A breeze caresses and wraps itself around and through the leaves and branches,
and coaxes a parting with its seed,
which suitably adorned, pirouettes in the wind's hands,
to land upon the ground somewhere below.
Where, by fate, it finds a home in the earth,
from whence it once drew its sustenance,
to transfigure now into a sapling.

A breeze caresses to distract,
and serves to deflect attention elsewhere;
diverted, amused, beguiled,
by whatever tact, to cause to wander and to stray away from truth and what is real,
and momentarily conceal what is,
for what is not.

A breeze caresses to turn the pages,
and from the words an idea and understanding forms.
Nebulous to start,
and then to gel,
it takes form, imperceptibly at first shape,
on its resultant way to fixed stance,
of what to believe, to say, to do.

A breeze caresses gently her face,
and with slight, and questioned hesitation,
pushes his toward hers,
under a dimmed light, cast from the night's orb,
peering overhead,
to meet.
Where by love, lips find lips,
and from lover's breath shared,
to become one in the moment,
forever more.

The Uprooted Purpose

The purposes that fuel the soul,
    and breathe life into life,
    into its myriad actions,
    the commitments to the purpose,
    and belief that the purposes are noble and real and true,
    to one such purpose was wedded an aspiration,
    to help shape it and adorn it and guard and gently guide it,
    to preserve its pure essence and integrity.
Then trodden upon,
    a suggestion, no an intent, that the purpose was to change,
    no, had to change,
    not because of honor or right or intentions well conceived,
    but spurred by weakness and short-sightedness and ambition.
The purpose changed,
    and as an insidious infestation,
    its leaves withered and spotted black.
    With little care,
    it faltered and morphed,
    into something different,
    short of scope and reason.
The soul no longer fueled,
    beliefs chopped and hacked to pieces,
    as a mirror shattered, strewn about in disregard,
    now faced with dilemma,
    to compromise and subsist,

    or to rise and seek new air to breathe,
    new purpose to nourish,
    one more noble and honest and true.
And so, the rotting,
        is uprooted and cast aside,
        to make way for breathing new life into life,
        a new purpose to feed the soul.

A Time to Kill

A time to kill anger
    blame
    callousness
    discrimination
    envy
    fear
    greed
    hatred
    ignorance
    jealously
    killing
    lying
    meanness
    negativity
    obstination
    pessimism
    quarreling
    rudeness
    selfishness
    temper
    unreliability
    violence
    worry
    xenophobia
    yammering
    zealotry.

To Heal

Her hand I held, as I took my first steps,
    to balance my gait,
    uncertain, unsteady,
    to show me how to walk.
Her hand I held, when I fell off my bike,
    to skin my knees,
    bleeding, crying,
    to calm me, while washing the wounds.
Her hand I held, when that first day of school,
    to walk with me the short distance,
    to the end of the street,
    to reassure that I was ready.
Her hand I held, when I was sick,
    to see how tired and febrile and weak,
    unwell to venture forth I felt,
    to comfort me and help heal me.
Her hand I held, when donned in cap and gown,
    to graduate,
    ending one phase in transition to the next,
    to tell me that she was proud of me.
Her hand I held on my wedding day,
    to walk to the center of the room,
    for our dance,
    to let me know she was happy for me.

Her hand I held,
    to share in my pure joy,
    in the gift of new life,
    to feel in that moment what she must have once felt.
Her hand I held the second to the last time,
    to walk with her in her confusion,
    recent memories gone,
    to be there in the moment of our together.
Her hand I held that last time,
    to watch her, eyes closed, slowly breathe,
    her last breaths and
    to not know if she knew her hand I held.
Her hand I can no longer hold,
    to mourn the loss,
    yet, in my heart and mind's memories, she still lives,
    to hold my hand and my self to be.

Tearing Down

Once upon a time,
    fairy-taled innocence passed,
    years of truths, whose lights are seen through clear waters,
    as they are,
    steady shown.
But the waters muddy and the lights
    fade away from view,
    replaced by the reflected trinity of
        ambitions, vanities and pride.
Its new light faux bright.
Its lure enticing.
Its scent intoxicating.
Its self applauded,
    and touted as success.
All that is worthwhile,
    all that is desired,
    all that is acclaimed,
    takes its queue and feeds from it.
Carefully, carelessly, knowingly, unknowingly,
    it entangles and ensnares.
Its vapors mist and
    surround,
    and becomes one
        with the air that is breathed.

It becomes part of who one is,
    and what one believes,
    and what one wishes for,
    and even whilst one sleeps, what dreams are dreamed.
The self that has been presumed built of brick and mortar,
    malaligned,
    believed tall and strong,
    leans as Pisa's tower.
As a top heavy tree blown this way and that,
    it risks the peril of being broken asunder,
    torn down.
Yet, if one can see through those muddied waters,
    the lights which once truly burned,
    once upon a time,
    still flicker.
Then the brick and mortar holds,
    straight and sure,
    and though currents may shift,
    it be for naught.

Built Upon

From the dappled reds and yellows and browns,
    leaves gathered to knit a pillowed pile,
    built upon the ground,
    toward it, I totter and fall,
    squealing in delight.
From the sands that are pulled by ebb and tide,
    shovel and bucket in tow,
    built upon the shore,
    a castle rises with towers and moat, and I
    reveling in the play.
From the flakes of snow that find their way down,
    with gloved hands,
    built upon the drifts, a man of sorts,
    a friend stands admiring him, now apparelled with buttons
        and hat,
    laughing with him in delight.
From the disassembled bars and frame and tires,
    the two-wheeled conveyance is assembled,
    built upon the wish to peddle and race and move,
    a new lease on life,
    speeding against the winds of new found freedom.
From the myriad of hours spent listening and reading and writing,
    time studying,
    built upon the goals to learn and to become,
    a degree is awarded,
    graduating me onto a life that had already started.

From the first hesitant, timid interactions,
    we met and grew,
    built upon trust and devotion and love,
    love realized and shared,
    vowing for better or for worse, we sealed our fates together.
From the first breaths and crying,
    our ones grew,
    built upon our shared affections,
    the brood flourished,
    changing ever, blossoming.
From lives led,
    and toils and labors and joys and failures shared,
    built upon the years, as they bound us,
    a home comes to be,
    creating a haven shared.
From the leaves which cushioned a life led,
    all that transpired so swiftly was
    built upon faith and hope,
    but not least of all, always,
    turning on love.

Season of Tears

The winds blow cold and leaves have colored, fallen and withered,
and snow visits the skies to carpet the world below.
In bitter cold gelid,
overcast heavens dim the feeble light which casts shadows
    over the austere setting.
During this season, expectancies glimmer and glow
in preparation for the remembrance of Him.

Dusted trees are shaken and brought inside,
dressed and ornamented,
swathed in lights and tinsel ostentatious.
Songs are carolled, hummed and chorused,
familiar strains from yesterdays.
Confections baked and bedecked,
with fruits and sugar coating.
Gifts wrapped with vivid colored papers,
tied and bowed with ribbons.
Tables set with china fine,
runners red and green and gold, and centered pieces florally
    adorned.

Howbeit, below the surface, surreptitious,
the season also occasions with it tears,
that may gently flow and rise
at unforeseen, chanced, feared or serendipitous moments.

The bauble reminds of a time past.
Melodic chords clutch and pull.
The sweets call up memories of laughtered days.
Presents evoke feelings of gratitude and elation.
A chair left desolate tableside remembers one loved.

Shades of Laughter

Laughter comes dressed in many guises.
    The guffaw at a joke well told.
    The chuckle of self-assured happiness.
    The chortle of a child excited in anticipation.
    The cackle of bliss when successful after much effort.
    The howl of delight at a prank well played.
    The roar of drunken hilarity.
    The ha-ha of polite approval.
    The breaking up when sharing in a joyous secret.
    The crack up at being discovered.
    The giggle at oneself for being reminded of how much a fool one is.
    The titter shared with an audience at a performance well done.
    The shriek of pure joy.

To Heal

What can be said in the moment,
    and what can be heard in the present,
    that assuages the sadness,
    quells the mourning, the grief,
    of being newly bereft of one who has become
    inextricably linked to one's being, one's soul?
After all, to lament is mortal.
To acknowledge the inevitability is grievous.
To heal takes time.
How does one begin to make sense of loss?
To make meaning from the void?
To grow accustomed to not hearing the voice?
Feeling the touch?
Reveling in the smile?
Embracing solace in the presence?
The sting burns and poisons in the instant.
Forthwith and insidiously, it overwhelms and blinds.
After all, to lament is mortal.
To acknowledge the inevitability is grievous.
To heal takes time.
But how does one mend?
To find the balm, the salve for what burns?
The relief, restoration, revival, renewal, retrieval, reclamation,
    recovery, resumption?
The resurrection of one's being?

After all, to lament is mortal.
To acknowledge the inevitability is grievous.
To heal takes time.
Just as losses are fated,
    so too are the seasons.
They persist and shift and come and go.
And so must one,
    persist and adapt.
To lean and be carried when we must,
    knowing that to support and carry in the future we would,
    when needed in return.
After all, to acknowledge the inevitable is grievous.
To heal takes time.
To rediscover that between our pains and our hurts and our losses,
    and our hopes,
    we must moor ourselves to what lies at our center, our home.
For there dwells love,
    with its aspirations and passions and whims and affections.
After all, to heal takes time.
And from the sadness can come the sweet,
    and yes, from the sweetness, a bit of sadness.
For although gone,
    tis not entirely so.
The voice, the touches, the smiles, the presence
    are the remembrances that abide with us,
    the mementos of all the good that there was and is.
And with these keepsakes fastened to our spirit,
    we heal,
        till which time our souls may embrace again.

The Dance

Tis wondrous solace found when hand meets hand,
    to lift ourselves and carry kindred souls
    toward the momentary center of our worlds.
Poised, anticipating the start of dulcet chords and notes
    that will gently move ourselves to glide across the open floors
    in deliberate concert.
Feeling storied measures guide our steps and turns,
    right, then left, and back to right,
    as if to float upon the air beneath.
Unbroken, rolling seamlessly from harmonious concord,
    mirroring the vicissitudes of our together,
    the syncopated rhythm of our journeyed lives danced as one.
The mere intrusion of a forgotten step causes but momentary pause,
    as strains continue and the tide resumes,
    tandem, together, tethered by one seamless burning light.
The world around forgotten in the moment,
    but remembered,
    as we surrender our ourselves cloaked in raptured bliss.
And as the surreptitiously approaching cadence of the music
    finds us,
    poised, the silence wraps its arms around us,
    twas heaven, the dance.

Scattered as One

Along the verge where the waters ever so gently roll to meet
    the sands,
    we venture with hands held,
    and gaze out to where the sky reaches down to touch
        the waters.
In our silence, our being there,
    the rhythmic sound of the loch reaching out toward us
        softly plays,
    broken by a gull's beckoning to join,
    to soar and glide above all.
The surface glistens, glimmers and glitters,
    its gleams conceal its depths, its unknowns,
    which rest shrouded below.
We pause, as we decide upon a stone,
    and cast it in unison upon the world before our visage
        toward what can not be seen,
    to watch it skip along the surface,
    until it skips no more.
And with each stone we scatter before us,
    we know not how it may dance
    and where it may finally find its rest,
    but we know that it is scattered as one.

Gathering Stones

The smiles that come with the simple pleasures.
The peace that comes with walking upon the sand.
The quiet that comes with sitting amongst the words.
The beauty that blooms with the flowers.
The calm that comes with the dawn.
The wonder of the stars in the night.
The joy that follows the laughter.
The tears that come with the joy.
The urge that comes to sway with the music.
The desire to sing the words of songs known.
The anticipation that follows tradition.
The sweetness of sugared treats.
The happiness that comes with first steps taken or words spoken.
The love that is shared in a kiss.
The rejoicing of hugs at reunions.
The fascination of learning things new.
The surprise of being pleasantly surprised.
The awe of mountains capped with snow.
The tranquility of being warm when it is cold.
The brilliance of the lights on a tree.
The pride of simple stories shared.
The appreciation of words listened to.
The elation of helping one in need.
The emotion of being helped when in need.
The blessings that are simple and often overlooked.

Embracing Dreams

There once was a man,
    not a famous man,
    not a man of wealth, or might, or power,
    by the measures of the men in his day.
He lived simply, unassumingly,
    working with his hands,
    building things with wood-
        places for people and animals to sleep and eat and live,
    tools with which to farm, to build and to make food,
    staffs with which to shepherd sheep or with which some
        might steady their gait,
    and small trinkets and toys for little ones to play with.
And in those rare moments, when the day's light was fading,
    and the day's work finished,
    he might take his blades to carefully carve a figure –
    a sheep which strayed from the pasture,
    or a donkey who lived in the stable nearby,
    or a bird that would be noticed, perched close.
He was a quiet man, a solitary man, shy some might say,
    who busied himself each day 'cept one.
One night as he slept,
    he dreamt of a man coming, as he worked.
He noticed the man for some reason, but could not recall why.
The man approached and sat nearby to watch as he worked.

He was conscious of being watched but feared to look up,
    at first,
        until the better part of curiosity caused him to stop,
        and glance up at the man who had been patiently watching.
The man smiled,
    as he did in response.
"Good man,
    I have watched you work,
    and your work is worthy."
"That is kind of you to say."
"I have a favor to ask."
"What may that be?"
"Could you craft for me with your hands and the wood a face
    of a woman?"
"Whose face may that be?"
"You will know.
    I will return in a fortnight to see her face."
"How will I know where to start?"
The man got up and slowly walked back in the direction from
    whence he appeared.
Once woke from the dream,
    he pondered on the man and the request for the next days.
During one such moment, as he walked to his plain abode,
    he happened upon a piece of wood from an olive tree,
        waiting along the road's side.
Feeling it of some value, he picked it up and inspected it.
    with its variegated shades of brown.
That evening by the light of his fire,
    whose flickering cast shadows all around him,
    he chiseled an image from the wood of a woman,
    not anyone he knowingly knew.

As the fire's flames faded,
> he set the piece upon a small stool outside his door,
> and there it sat waiting for the fortnight to come.

When the day dawned,
> a young woman with her mother happened by the house,
> and gave notice to the figure.

The mother stopped and stared for a bit at the face
> and recognized the visage.

She looked to see if the man who carved the face was there,
> but he was not.

Later toward sunset, she returned alone to find him there,
> seated by a fire.

"Excuse me.
> I have noticed your work,
> and its appearance is quite familiar to me.
> The image you have crafted with your hands
> > looks very much like my daughter."

He looked at her, uncertain.

"Do you know her from somewhere?"

"I do not believe I do,
> as I do not know you."

"The face is remarkably the same."

Silence ensued,
> after which, he coyly inquired,
> > "Would you mind terribly to bring her by that I may see her face?"

She nodded. "I will return in the morrow at this time."

That night he dreamt again of the man,
> who approached from the darkness that was descending around,
> > to carefully inspect the face.

"Tis her face you crafted."
"Whose face?
    I know not this woman."
"Not yet, but you shall.
    To you in the morrow she shall come with her mother."
"How do you know this?
    And what do I do?"
"You shall know what to do when the time comes."
He rose and slowly walked back into the night,
    leaving the sculptor to ponder these things.
The next day came, and with it, the mother with her daughter.
Her hand,
    he eventually asked for in marriage,
A child,
    she conceived that was not his,
    and he vowed to quietly leave her,
    but another dream brought the man,
    who told him to have faith,
    and to stay.
In the night,
    by star's light,
    in a shelter built by his hands,
    the child, who was not, yet who was, his,
    came into the world.
From thence forward, the man,
    who was not so famous,
    not wealthy, or mighty, or so powerful,
    by the measures of the men in his day,
    became someone much more,
    by humbly embracing his dreams.

Far From the Embrace

Temptation, quietly poised,
    stares unabashedly,
    surreptitiously, making itself known.
    coaxing, ever so coyly,
    that it may gain notice.
It innocently pleads,
    to lure your attention for just a brief moment,
    from what you know is the right,
    the rule, the law, the truth.
Its presence baits and whets and draws,
    to see the other,
    to look past dissuasions, remonstrations, and expositions.
After all, they will always be there,
    for this once,
    just this once,
    this brief and fleeting moment.
With hands extended,
    it invites
    to be allured,
    enticed,
    fascinated,
    captivated,
    bewitched,
    wheedled,
    coaxed,

    and charmed,
    animated as a metal to its magnet,
    pulled and drawn to it.
Arms outstretched,
    it beckons,
    and asks to embrace for but a moment or two or more.
The choice to do so or remain afar in the balance –
    to be tipped.

Seeking in the Shallow Depths

Peering askance into the rippled watered mirror
at reflections cast
and seen through narrow eyes,

we watch as peoples pass
into and out of view,
crossing their reflections with ours.

The scowls, the peace,
the downcast eyes and beaming smiles,
the frightened, happy, angry and calm are seen.

We hasten to frame and hang the visages
against our reflection
and no further thoughts give them.

What is lost in the watered depths,
beyond the surface,
the opaque side of the mirror,

are the losses, the struggles,
the heartaches and pains,
the angers, hurts, frustrations and sorrows.

They float in the shallow depths
just under the reflection
where they preside.

We oft not consider or seek
beyond the reflections of the rippled watered mirror,
as we stroll past, peering at our own reflections.

Lost

Along the road I traveled,
    in my disillusioned way,
    with map in hand to guide me true.
The path so planned,
    its destination believed so clear and set.
Diligently, I walked,
    keeping to the course I set.
The goals were clear,
    my pack weighted heavy,
    with tasks to spend along the way,
    aimed so well to keep me on the narrow,
    as my compass so directed,
    and as my aspirations beckoned.
For many a mile, I trod,
    along the road,
    doused in rain,
    trudging though the mud,
    tracking up and down the hills.
But all was well,
    for ambition and drive were my journey's companions,
    quite convincing and engaging.
Then quite a length along the way,
    with the journey almost ended,
    the course was blocked and dammed,

    the path obstructed,
    the passage forward was no more,
    the long and mighty trek abruptly halted.
With purposes and motives tethered, trapped,
    pursuit forbidden and no longer blessed,
    the reasons now lay like lead upon the road,
    all tangled in confusions,
    and cloaked in anger and frustrations,
    and blinded by regrets.
I paused and gazed around,
    lost now as to the way,
    to discover an opening, so small, in the wood,
    that had defined the road on which I'd travelled.
Faced with choice,
    back I turned to stare from whence I came,
    and then to fruitlessly wallow, where I stood, in fate's
        aborted glare.
From there, I hesitantly turned,
    and chose the narrow gap between the trees,
    which appeared to end in darkness,
    and meandering I went,
    in the narrow between the trunks,
    over fallen logs and branches,
    and boulders hidden by the leaves.
With no apparent direction,
    I moved and blindly trusted,
    until the tight and incommodious path
    widened into a larger way,
    better lit and purposed than before,
    aimed in another direction,
    toward another destination.

And along that road I now travel,
    this new, once unbeknownst way,
    the end perhaps less clearer,
    but the burden feeling lighter,
    and the time and moment right,
    for with me on the road now,
    travel faith and hope.

Things to Keep

Keep focus on that which is most important in life.
Heap kindness and gratitude upon those whom you meet.
Leap past those who are ruled by the negative.
Seep and let the small joys in life find their way to you.
Creep past your insecurities and have faith.
Deep dive past petty ambitions and grab hold of that which
    is noble.
Bleep out the crass and the vulgar as you speak.
Sleep, knowing you did all of your best that day.
Clepe out motives that are worth the while.
Cheap be not with your gratefulness.
Kreep and other rare treasures keep close to your heart
Sweep away those things that are not necessary.
Leep not at every small trouble and stay calm.
Peep through the crevices and the cracks for what is true.
Reap the joys of true happiness by listening to others.
Steep yourself in fortitude to venture out of your comfort.
Threap those who bully others who are vulnerable.
Asleep, do not, when those around you are distressed.
Cheep happiness each day to those who you greet.
Sheep and other timid beings, to them be gentle.
Beep to signal others that you are ready to help.
Aheap efforts to build upon your accomplishments.
Keep focus on that which is good and on that which is right.

Time to Cast Away

Why is it
    that so easily,
    and so quickly,
    a problem can be seen,
    and its pain felt,
    and its hurt anchors upon the mind?
Why is it
    that so easily,
    it is to dwell on misfortune,
    to make one's home,
    upon the mishaps, and reverses,
    and the sorrows?
Why is it
    that so well versed,
    and rehearsed are we,
    to sit and wallow in,
    the fortunes broken?
Why is it
    that so drawn are we,
    to failures past and forecasted,
    and hardships shadowed,
    by the clouds and buffeted by ill-winds?

Why is it
> that upon the fears,
> we feed in frenzied rapture,
> seemingly never to have our fill,
> always hungering for more?

Why is it
> that so slowly,
> and oft with such hesitation,
> we seek
>> to find the peace?
>> to seek the strength?
>> to count the blessings?
>> to cast away the burdens?
>> to lighten what weighs upon the soul?

Torn

Gone.
Was the only utterance
that was heard.
Breaths all breathed.
In the silence that now,
engulfed the room,
and wrapped itself around,
as a garment fitted too small,
rent in anguish
from top to bottom.
The still hand held,
afraid to part,
lest its warmth fade away,
forever, as is destined.
Visage blurred,
as waters swell and surge,
unrelenting, as they flow and fall.
Convulsive sounds emerge
from the depths, and wrack the body and the soul,
uncontrolled, unfettered, freed, and true.
Held abeyant for so long,
knowing this moment would come
to pass, and yet,
praying, and hoping, it would not.
And in the moment,
anguish overwhelms, and finally, without intention,
the hand releases to clutch the self.

The Quilt

The quilt I sew
With each moment,
Imperfect though it is,
The memories selected
The unique fabric chosen,

is stitched with what
it slowly takes its shape,
it is all of my doing,
and pieced together
the colors that are picked,

I do each day.
begins to form a pattern.
its imperfections are mine.
to create the work are mine.
its design is one of a kind.

The pieces are placed
Overall, there seems
Yet, upon closer inspection,
seemingly unrelated portions
juxtaposed and placed,

in position in what appears
a purpose to the arrangement,
each piece appears discrete,
positioned next to patches
to weave a tapestry mine,

to be an ordered way.
a simplicity to the construct.
bits assembled together,
that uniquely blend,
peculiar, custom, idiosyncratic.

The pieces that come
consist of the myriad of
Births and deaths,
illusions and certainties,
reflections and impulses,

together, in a random,
occasions past and present
triumphs and failures,
struggles and ease,
serendipity and deliberate,

variegated, yet ordered way,
and those yet to happen.
happy times and sad,
laughter and weeping,
excitement and ennui.

These things that cause
cause one to pause
to go from here.
what we decide to do,
and all that we hope,

us to move and to grow
and stand in uncertainty,
It is this checkered quilt
and what we believe,
that ever wraps around

and those things that
what to do and where
of who we are and
and what we value,
and holds us.

In the Absence of a Silence

Each day we wake
to the noise and the din of the routine
with its ever churning
turning ways
pulling us tither
and to hither
incessantly
beckoning us to do
this one thing
and the others
simultaneously
or in rapid fire succession
demanding that we give attentions
to the now
and to what is yet to come
convincing ourselves that we must act
or react
to talk when we need to
or when we ought not
but feel compelled to do so
to make a point
or take a stand
that melds with our agendas
our priorities
our ever prime concerns

since such issues
have oft come with much consideration
and careful plotting
or may be dressed as whims transient
as we roam along our days
and weeks and years
seeking
for attentions
to be heeded
and noticed
the mind swirling
tracked in forethoughts
strategizing
to at times be derailed
by fires
passions ranging wide
from elated places high
to the abyss.

In the midst of our own cacophonies,
and in the absence of a silence,
we take no notice that we can not hear
each other.

We Speak

We speak
as part of days past.
Part of all that was done.
Part of all that was met.
Heirs to the customs and the folklores,
a mosaic of all those who came before,
whose lives were lived,
and parts of themselves bequeathed to us.
We start not from nothing.
The oft unknown lives of those seen no more
endure in us and in those to come.

We speak
as part of days present.
Part of all that is done.
Part of all that we meet.
Nothing that is done affects only the self.
Power is wielded to create joy,
as is the power to elicit sorrow.
The command to engender good,
and the sway to promote what is not good.
Deeds done move not only us,
but all those whose paths we cross.

We speak
as part of what is to come.
Part of all that will be done.
Part of all that will be met.
As we have gleaned from the past,
we pay forward to the future,
to the children and their children.
We bestow pieces of who we were,
and small parts of what we did,
to become part of those who follow,
a link in the chain connecting our past to what is to come.

Love is...

Patience, when angers foment,
    and hurt seizes to torment.
Perseverance, when it is easier to quit,
    and when challenges seem greater than the fit.
Constancy, when the vicissitudes of life creates illusions of unstable,
    and when misfortunes seem to enable.
Steadiness, when the course seems unsure,
    and when emotions prevail and obscure.
Persistence, toward that which is right and good,
    and doing what one knows one should.
Tenacity, for honor and what is truth,
    and not to acquiesce to whims of youth.
Endurance, to hold firm and fast to love,
    and recognize its strength over and above.
Courage, to persist in one's convictions,
    despite assaults and admonitions.
Tranquility, to stop and breathe and be at peace,
    when all the noise around will not cease.
Serenity, to accept those things we can not change,
    and the strength to move on those that we can rearrange.
Calmness, when all the world seems to shout,
    or when all around mope and pout about.
Quiet, to be alone with our tranquility,
    and sometimes to allow commotions to clamor with humility.

Fortitude, when tragedy comes unexpected and descends,
    and the strength to accept the help of friends.
Forbearance, when tossed and turned by the tides of life,
    those trials that lead to stress and strife.
Contentment, at the end of each day,
    that you did your best along the way.

Hatreds Taught

With dimpled cheeks and childhood grin,
and chocolate smeared upon the chin,
perched upon a knee and smiling,
too young, too innocent to be guiling,
inquisitively staring off in space,
then turning toward the wizened face.

Tell me why some people's skin is dark,
and why the color calls to hark,
for some believe that that mark,
gives cause to treat that one with snark?

And why I see some boys do bully,
those in dresses, skirts, so fully,
to the point of tears and bitter crying,
so that they feel like they must be dying?

For why those bedecked in expensive wear,
with pricey toys and clothes with flair,
frown and laugh at those with little,
as if their worth was but a tittle?

And tell me how it comes to be,
that those who came from far across the sea,
who can not speak our language yet,
are mocked and posited as a threat?

Why those who pray in a certain way,
who believe or do not believe as they may,
find a different way so undoubtedly wrong,
and deciding for that they do not belong?

And what comes to make some believe,
that the old and gray can not retrieve,
thoughts of any weight or worth,
or ideas with much of any girth?

And then those with a misshaped face,
or body contour of great disgrace,
so readily ignored or mercilessly teased,
since they differ from that which pleased?

What was one to answer to the queries posed,
that differences are often presupposed,
to be somehow lesser and to be hated,
and perhaps such sentiments are fated,
to be born from actions demonstrated,
and from the lessons we are taught,
when we were little and supposedly knew naught?

Time of War

We sat, together,
    across from one another,
    and he looked down at the ground which lay between us,
    and his words at first came slowly.
Warily, as by my nature,
    for nature is directed by the past,
    I approached,
    skeptically,
    cautiously,
    and listened,
    interested in what was being said,
    in the vision of what was promised and could be.
I came to believe in so listening,
    that there might be a better way,
    a more authentic way,
    a more honest way,
    a more enlightened way,
    a kinder way.
I was invited to become part of this something new,
    something different.
And with cares set aside,
    a willingness to try this something took me,
    this something new and maybe better,
    and I agreed to join.

The start came after much planning,
> and with it, I climbed into a boat,
> one of many boats,
> and taking up the oars,
> I commenced rowing with the others,
> following the lead,
> promised and promising that there was shore,
> at the other end of the water's body,
> but not being able to see it.

Knowing that the course taken might be anything but straight,
> and the waters would at times
> rock the boat and those carried by it,
> upon reflections and with resolve,
> I rowed,
> making the journey,
> believing in its purpose and the promise.

Naysayers lined the shores, as we departed,
> and pontificated,
> clamoring that it could not be done
> since it had not been done before,
> it was different from what is currently done
> and therefore
> it was wrong,
> and it was preposterous to think it could
> at all work.

And so, I followed,
> hoping the pull
> would give way to truth,
> and as I labored,
> I gained in strength and conviction,
> and I found myself,

toward the front,
where from, I even helped at times to guide,
and steer direction.
My goals were their goals.
My values, their values.
My morals, their morals.
My faith, their faith.
And so things went for a while,
and with passing time,
they became part of who I was,
what moved me,
what nurtured me,
what gave me home.
And I even came to think,
that it might be conceivable,
to be part of the future,
to perhaps lead the course,
to preserve and protect,
what had been intended,
and what had become.
But, as more time passed,
those that created the vision and led the way,
disembarked from the journey.
And hoping to ascend,
lifted by what I believed…
He paused as he was speaking,
to find the words,
which followed.
What was not known,
or perhaps, believed could be,
was that other agendas were at play,
and others who did not know the way,

      but thought they did,
      rose to rank by plans, predesigned and conceived,
      who behind a façade of words,
      led astray by subtlety,
      and at times not so subtle,
      with aggressions tossed.
And to me and others was pronounced, and oft then denied,
      that your skin is not the color that is right for this, but
           it is good for that,
      your religion fringe,
      your dress makes for discomfort,
      your background too pedestrian and different,
      your love of your life too queer,
      your appearance and behavior too strange,
      your thoughts differ and do not agree.
To the depths, they tore,
      and from those depths inside, rose a war,
      within my soul,
      with aspirations crushed and dashed,
      and hopes pushed aside.
Old truths that perhaps always lay below,
      found their voices once again,
      in insecurities and pride,
      to rule those who cowered and paid homage to them.
Direction shifted by the storm
      of ambition,
      and values changed.
For that which had once been envisioned and realized,
      and hoped to be a new truth, or a new day,
      quickly blurred and was dismissed by
      delusions, illusions, deceptions and avoidances.

But it was in me that the war waged,
> for the fool I had thought I had been,
> to blindly believe.

And for wont of oars to now steer,
> and for the loss of way,
> to persist?
> to quit?
> to change?
> to adapt?
> to acquiesce?
> to compromise?
> to defy or accept?
> to anger?
> to mourn?

He stopped his story,
> *seemingly quagmired in an entanglement of questions,*
> *or as if the story was at a loss for where to then go.*

And I inquired of him,
> *what he then did.*

After a bit, he straightened himself,
> *and looked at me for the first time in telling.*

To fight a battle lost,
> I opted not.

Perhaps I should have been the braver,
> and persisted to try and change,
> but such seldom changes.

And so quietly,
> I wrested myself up out of the boat,
> and placed the oars along the side for someone else,
> who might not be deterred by what was old.

Holding onto the conviction that not all ventures taken are
 necessarily lost,
 that in each journey lies both that which is good,
 and that which is not,
 and that truth and hopes can live, as I had seen,
 must live,
 despite,
 I declared an end to this battle,
 and walked away,
 toward another peace.

Pax Vobiscum

One day will come to pass,
    when part of me will leave you,
    to set out from here,
    and rejoin those who have gone before.
And in those moments which are to follow,
    I leave with you a few small notions,
    as bits of consolation,
    to wrap their arms around you,
    and hold you ever so closely and dearly,
    as if I were still with you.
And please remember,
    there will unfailingly and always,
    be a part of me which will hold you so.
Be kind to each other,
    and to those who you meet,
    and know or may not know.
    We all carry the burdens of our journeys,
        as weights upon our shoulders,
        and such affections,
        at moments which you may not know,
        will make a difference.
    Be kind even when some others,
        accuse you of insincerity, or selfishness,
        or of having covert designs,
        for in the end,
        it is not between you and these others, who think
            and speak so.

Love,
    and clutch and cling to those who are truly near to you.
    Be brave enough to freely let them be close,
        even when temptations whisper,
        that you should pull away,
        or bar their entrance to your heart and soul.
    Let them ever be so nigh,
        that the very thought of losing them,
        or their agonies or struggles,
        cause you so much grief and worry,
        for they are a better part of who you are,
        and despite all,
        will provide true strength and solace.
Believe in yourself and who you are,
    and what you have done,
    and what you will do,
    especially, if from the heart.
    Do not let other's words or actions discourage you,
        from doing what is right,
        and what is good.
    For you have in you,
        capacity to do great things with great love,
        and in the end,
        that makes those things and the doer of those things,
        worth believing and trusting in.
Permit yourself peace,
    whatever that may be for you.
    Peace to live each of the precious moments you have in
        the moment.
    To let go of all the inconsequential.
    To enjoy being with those you love.

To savor the walk on the shore, or in the woods,
   in the snow, or amidst the falling colored leaves, or
      fields in bloom.
To immerse yourself in the words of another, or in prayer,
   or in the notes of song.
To raucously celebrate the joyous and good in life.
And always and forever
   may your faith be unwavering,
   until we meet again in another place,
   of perfect peace.

www.ingramcontent.com/pod-product-compliance
Lightning Source LLC
LaVergne TN
LVHW011740060526
838200LV00051B/3270